NIGHTSHIFT
Erika Burkart

AN AREA OF SHADOWS
Ernst Halter

*Translated from the German
by Marc Vincenz*

*Spuyten Duyvil
New York City*

Publication of this volume is in part made possible by ProHelvetia, the Swiss Arts Council. **pr∂helvetia**

"An Early Morning in Daylight-Saving Summer" was previously published in *Guernica*. "Reflections" was previously published in *Hyperion Journal*.

Library of Congress Cataloging-in-Publication Data

Burkart, Erika, 1922-2010.
  [Nachtschicht. English]
  Nightshift / Erika Burkart. An Area of Shadows / Ernst Halter Ernst Halter ; translated from the German by Marc Vincenz.
    pages cm
  ISBN 978-0-923389-06-2
  I. Halter, Ernst. Area of Shadows. II. Title. III. Title: Area of Shadows.
  PT2662.U68N3313 2013
  831'.914--dc23
                        2013005702

Nightshift
Erika Burkart

An Area of Shadows
Ernst Halter

This book is a conversation between two poets—one dying, the other very much alive—attempting to come to terms with death and dying, with life and living on.

Nightshift represents the dying poet's final words. Written over a period of two years, scribbled in notebooks and on scraps of paper, from her deathbed (much was written in the middle of the night or the earliest hours of the morning), Erika Burkart scrutinizes herself with a knife-edged clarity and reluctantly accompanies herself into "the chasm"—as long as words materialize and the hand obeys.

The process of writing these poems was perhaps the only thing that helped her hold on to the last ragged strands of her life—she had been ill for many years. She never quite managed to finish the manuscript. Ernst Halter, her life- and literary-partner, transcribed, decoded, and finalized the manuscript. In the second section of the book, An Area of Shadows, fellow-poet, Ernst Halter, bids farewell to companion and deepest friend for more than forty years.

Seldom has such a poetic conversation taken place.

Schaffhausen, Switzerland
November 30, 2012

Marc Vincenz

Nightshift
Erika Burkart

Shifted Towards the Inside

Exposed

Lost Words – Lost World

Nemo

An Area of Shadows
Ernst Halter

Nightshift
Erika Burkart

Shifted Towards the Inside

DISTANCES

The barren spells
always longer,
the joy a full stop,
the love a spark
extinguished in flight.
Where he dwindled,
a black star
recalled the axis
of one's heart—
as distant
as celestial spheres.

AN OLD PERSON'S JOY AND FRUSTRATION

If every word
is a story,
writing to addresses
that no longer exist—
being alone with almost everything
one still loves,
pointless questions consider:
Who are you? Where do you come from?
Giving pearls, clothes and books,
and also—incomplete, those writings
of deep pain and the nightly sea.

To recognize oneself in old photos,
recalling the shy child.
To wave goodbye,
chew tablets, imbibe tasteless tea
as a love potion.
With lies to soothe the worries
of those left behind,
their suffering
on our final departure.

Wind

Nomad from afar who doesn't know us, wind,
my most alien element,
until the tide eases itself into the wave.

Once, at high tide,
what a glimmer on the threshold:
it seemed impenetrable, in that space
beyond the entire world.

You loved me,
I loved you—
love: dust that scattered above and away
in the June light—
when the green hills and the soaring sky give us
what we can't comprehend.

Nor did I miss the hour
where my memory rests,
frozen solid, blinded, awakens,
vision learns through cosmic nights and days;
elementary
under your breath, Nomad.

And even when you bluster
in sleet and hard rain,
morning birds still soar toward you.

THE LONELY CHILD

Unwilling to begin the day,
I swallow three pills.
The hours falter, the hours trickle,
midday cloudy, evening red—
I'm still not dead, not without
those transforming memories
that I was once more than air and manure,
that I could speak,
write and read,
loved man and animal,
glass and stone, mist-creatures,
gentle trees too, earth's
most powerful, mortal dreams.
The child wished to become one of them
when she sat in the grass, above her the tree,
birds, sky, and from the sea—
such was the tale of the first book she read alone,
the all-knowing wind emerging—
unimaginable to soul and eye—
out of that star-, sun- and god-space.

Remembering

Grazed by a fleeting light,
the continually transmuting angel memory;
try to spell it out and it dissolves,
becomes cloudform, ambiguous, a hologram
of your own transience.

Memory-gap, memory-shock,
memory-panic, memory-fade;
deception and forgery; magnifying glass.
Smeared to an incompatible notion
rearranged from various dreams,
flaming gold; crude block of ore
from years unknown.

The Erinyes,
angel memory.
The woe of a healing wisdom?

Memory-addiction, memory-escape.
People forever tethered
together through memories,
through never-forgotten unforgiving enemies.
Forgetting. A drop of the old magic
still has its effect: irresistible, elective
affinities. And, in the second face,
that state of having-once-been-on-earth,
in a lightning-sharp,
mildly dull, painful light.

MAN IN THE MOON

What minds know,
numbers denominate.
You forget it. Forget it.
The moment mesmerizes you; now!
When after the hour
of late walkers and stretching shadows,
Miegel emerges breath upon breath
at the east gate,
man in the moor,
man in the moon, becoming children-
becoming crone-face,
when the child looked upward
at the mirror broken over and over.

Eye to Eye

I hear, said the woman,
the moon rising. A distant surge,
what one hears but doesn't see,
a stillness as it pushes upward from dark valleys,
as it chimes down from forested heights.
My old ears hear differently,
my streaky lights see other things,
mix up time of day and seasons,
blurred fragments and burning happiness.

Which time does the moon chime?
My time.
My oeuvre a wound;
my second snuffs out in unconsciousness
overtaking me, backwards and gently.
They say I have been sleeping!
Book and glasses on the floor—
I don't recall a thing,
sleep or wakefulness or reading.
Did you dream? No, no dream; I awoke
empty, a stalk
hollowed out until
it's nothing more than husk,

attempt to get a fix on life lived,
organize the overlooked
in the senseless chaos of the nearby,
to ward off specters of words,
not to curse. Worry.

The moon climbs crookedly
out of the hill onto the land,
where on Sundays, a thousand years ago,
as the mother was rubbing glasses clear
behind the counter, the child
stood chest-high in the grass,
eye to eye with flowers.

At the Trees

Where the linden tree and the fir
were closely related to you,
the leaf grew into your hand
and looked like a heart.
Sister linden!—needle upon needle,
fir and pine mirrored.

Trackless over the corn and the snow,
the bell found its way to the house
whose windows eyed the trees,
that recognized me
when I came home from afar.

Crowns of branches
grew in the trees;
and in their protective shadows
the woman was dwarfed, felt
reclined against the trunk of a walnut tree,
human form,
with her ever-narrowing body.

In front of the open door,
admittance permitted to those missing
and dead in my life, drive forth
black leaves from the twilight in late autumn,
finger words
to find their missing meanings,
coincide with sense and image, transformed
into a word found again.

REFLECTIONS

Reflections on books and the wall
from the lights of distant land.
Sheet-lightning. She shuns the mirror,
combs—while reflecting inside—
thoughts and hair. A shrug—
recalls the year of the drought,
that crinkle of flashes and sparse dry grass.

Last luminescence. The groan,
reflections, and the mirror now gone,
growing shadows detach
the old house from its roots.

Rain shower. After 11, this side
of twilight, the guests of the late hour.
They clear the table, have plenty of time,
know the place where one wrote and ate,
and before the eyes what was at hand,
gazed into the distance,
spun the yarn of meaning in the blue book
from here to there. The shepherdess read,
courageously in her magical shyness,
with bears and wolves, dwelt in caves,
and every animal loved
was made a rightful prince.

Being or non-being.
An old-new word,
can't be forgotten
when one speaks within the dark,
all alone with oneself.

TALKING AND EAVESDROPPING

You have a way with language
and conversations—as if you knew her,
as if she knew you—
weave in and out of
syllables and tones,
believe, through phrases, you're able
to see what writers saw,
though little is said when spoken,
except for those
ever-darkening questions.

With simple and complex sentences
you imprison the great hush,
eavesdropping on that murmur of stillness.
And in that listening,
behind sighs and syllables, sensing the invisible,
the true man.

The book as testament: old rhymes
like bridges that carry you
through the landscape and time
of the unborn, of the vanished—
quite true, and rather curious.

THE TRUTH ABOUT FAIRY TALES

Those who love each other are in serious danger.

The personal has remained.
If there's a soul, a mouth
that expresses fairy tales as if it
had been there when beggars were kings,
years were longer and trees charmed,
when birds were all-knowing
and ghosts and genies all on our side,
when above and below the earth
animals spoke our language,
exposed, carried away
through omnivorous time,
scattering memories and oblivion—

Those who love each other are in serious danger.

WAYSIDE CRUCIFIX IN WINTER

The stone crucifix. An almost-naked,
upright dead man in the frosty night.
He hung and suffered—
the child greeted him,
when she, a returning acquaintance, yet foreign,
secretly walked through the common
to go home in the evening,
a nocturnal creature along the wall—
and in the morning,
traces of prints in the snow.

Path's Edge Leading to the Mountain Forest

A path; in time
shifted inward.
I can still walk along it,
walk it alone.

Springtime.
Mountains of snow; nothing but snow,
formidable and towering over the path's edge,
its patchy fleece.

The earth opens its eyes
in gentian stars,
blue, the essence of dreams
one dreams before one awakens
into a life of icy cramps, and during summers
obscured in melancholia,
ripped apart by night storms.

I move, look—
shaking myself free of winter's nightmares—
flowers, risen,
first from the stone,
then from the ice.

SNOWED IN, ONE EVENING

They're all here. Waiting.
Snow hares, marmots,
the white crow, the crèche lamb,
brother deer, all
far from the spectral-eyed owl
and the hunter with the bone club.

The snow angel cowers back into the hedge,
the all-knowing book
under that narrow slung cloth;
jangling splinters of ice in the hedgerow
blot out his face.

The light is in the book—,
since night encroaches upon the wall,
the all-erasing shadow drawing near,
and flocculent seeds from the sinking sky
settle in forests, in pathless expanses.—
From the frost-rigid wings of fir trees,
the head of a horse: animal that thinks
he lost his rider
on the frozen moor,
striated by the blood of legends.

FRAGMENT

The shard.
Between the cracks
conjecture and inkling germinate—
if the reader shuts the book,
continues to spin the broken yarn,
ignores the empty spaces, patches them
with his own patterns and presumptions.

A fragment is read
differently in every epoch.
We work in the timely,
interpret, add and combine,
become aware—at the outermost corners,
in the innermost gaps,
proliferate the vague and the skew—
alarm and dupe.

What disturbed the reader's sleep
was someone awakened, observing, unbearably precisely,
who could see behind and ahead,
for which the earthly hour did not suffice;
and what is resolved in sidereal time—
once in the light and never again—

The shard: none
can finish the other
at that point which is the center—

Exposed

Sea

Madness
to want to tell of the sea.
Only the marooned, the bards, and seafolk
may write about the sea—
in their smooth talk, their lies, ordain it in myths,
proclaim it in silence; but the sea
has no language, is steadfast, in denial,
in salvation, is mother and death. The sea,
chessboard and battlefield of winds,
gathers, a deep, looming sky,
a mirror vibrating in waves of breath,
every shore in its picture,
where stars are like fishes,
fishes swimming like stars
glimmer black-silver—faun-like foreign creatures,
goggling many-eyed; a fire-tail
out of languid, fanning primordial weed,
eloquent in the world's universal tongue, silence.

Eavesdropping on this ancient chant of stillness,
I hear my own breathing and—
far over the cliffs within the cirque—
the wheeze, the slurp, the roar and blare,
the licking of the waves. No one truly arrives.
Beyond cries, lost in the storm,
while others are cooing at my feet;
and when the tides return,
the world's morass clears itself to the bottom.

The earth hurts; and we, her voice,
complain of how we've faulted her;
when twilight moves across our lips
like tender rain, our brows pale
when the flood reaches us in its surges—
and, from the beginning, not to be voiced,
from unutterable depths,
that deep sea-clang.

On a Sea Angel

(designed by the Irish landscape artist, Timothy O'Neill)

From all that far-into-the-distance staring
our eyes are out of focus
for inspecting close up,
and our ears deaf
when the wise wind whispers among the reeds.

I'm huddled at the stoneman's feet,
traveling with him over the crests,
ahead of me on the roundabout route to those
who once lived with me.

"Keep to the West,"
says the voice above the clouds,
"there you shall find the missing ones
in the galleries of the mountain,
where they concern themselves with the black flowers:
Rosa nigra" the stoneman is well aware,
storm birds taught him
the rage of the waves—, stillness,
purest silence and suffering.

THE OTHERS

Botanists, gardeners, poets
cannot solve the flowers' riddle.
Flowers are within their own rights,
survive farmers'
and state architects' pogroms,
possess roots that recall.

In that similar fruit-and-grub-
considered creation, the flower
is other, blooms incidentally,
is and wants to be beautiful,
relinquishes the semblance
of fulfilling duty and mission
except as healing herb, as an adornment,
is lust, ravishing, invents
sweet and deadly poisons,
seduces, unsettles, repels
with scents and has its way
with Eros and Thanatos.

Love-flower. Blooms for its own pleasure,
sea- and air-blue, is blind, but seems to see.
A consciousness of light in the absence of men,
when dawn unfolds.
Star, bell, chalice, umbel and sun.
No one knows when the Garden of Eden
watered the first seedlings, presented
the first buds to the sky.
From spring to spring I relearn
their apt and mythical names.
I peer into their golden eyes:
they look at me—as if they knew me, heard me,
strolling over the chasm.

TIME OF BLOOMING TREES

The feast lasts three to eleven days.
They are apparitions,
balls of light, plant luminaries.
Amazing! Behold!
looking upward in awe—already too late in the field,
the wonder has slipped by.
Space billows in snow,
blooms whirl as flakes
through the dull cold air,
settle themselves, are snow,
the party's over,
the light-tree extinguished the tree light;
you can't comprehend, seek comfort
in the soft seed-green: recognize
on the smoky-grey bark the first leaves
in your native garden—
from a distance, high in the sky,
the cherry tree blooms like a cloud,
an enraptured stranger, even under the clouds,
God knows who he's showing himself to,
on which mountain he will ignite his last spark;
when he fades, he shall darken
in a timeless twilight hour,
to remind us that the earth
was once a paradise,
and we, love-thirsty and drunk on blossoms,
were his guileless guests.

October Moon, Morning, 7:15 a.m.

A blister, watery red
over the western horizon,
as the fog rises over the moor
the pale morning moon submerges.

Awoke with a dark feeling; forgot
the dream. Was it a time-dream?
a sluggish? a torrential river?
You don't remember anything anymore. You weep.
Weeping,
you peel yourself from the night.

Arriving, looking, departing.
Did I see Ice Age glaciers,
moraines, Lindos the lake,
mirror of the mountain, the blood-moon?

Wasn't a soul there to see them.

Early Mist

Early autumn. Soon it will be dawn.
In the misty twilight
flakes release themselves, singular and sparse,
from the bleary-eyed branches,
spill, drip
in the morning breeze
over the wet grey-green meadow,
recall the blooms of the blackthorn,
bed themselves noiselessly,
blinking on the old leaves of the linden tree: scattered hearts.

Something crystalline vibrates
in spiders' webs,
flashes and shimmers—, expiring,
when the misty-wet-damp drives itself
down into the roots of the sapling,
nurturing the forest of the grandchildren.

END OF OCTOBER

Cloud castles. The sky is deep,
the sky is high, clear blues;
Foehn-storms and climactic lows
confuse men, birds and cattle.

A time of blazing trees, battered
in the storm during the night.
Crows rut in the stripped furrows,
an edgeless floor chambered by fog,
darkening after five; all-souls country.

In the sopping wet grass, apples rot,
picked unripe, they never ripen.
"Ripeness, the storeroom of death."

First frost. They clear out
the old stove, they shove
sprigs and tufts into the witches' hole.

The autumn day—"autumn-power-muffled",
resting and flowing,
just as it came about
for the child,
in a poem the first time—
it escapes in the afternoon vapors, washed blank,
the shine and transfiguration of the evening meadows.

[Autumn Leaves]

Shriveled, they resemble roots and animals,
old and young,
a diorama of memory.
Rilke notes they fall, "as if from afar,"
fall from their into our loneliness,

tumble and dangle.
Late in the year, they have
their own season,
bloom golden in October,
yellow as sunlight in early November,
and in the dark December, robbed of their color, they pale.
Autumn leaves, dead or alive.
In their blooming cloak they receive both.
Umbral autumn, night storm.

And how they nod,
the little birds—that pecking nuisance.
Beneath mosses, lichens and bark
tiny deaths occur,
their beastly, deadly tremors.
Only the thirteen-legged spiders
navigate the wide grid, achieve distance
with their devious stealth.

Their farewell gestures are tender.
They prepare themselves, disengage themselves,
scatter into White Hell's hair filaments,
into her ancestral lap,
console themselves with the soaring light.
They don't yet know of the White Death.

The old woman stares into the face of one
she no longer recognizes, one she once called
friend, considers the bread
she ate alone
for days, for years in the cold cell.

At the pond, maple and larch
burn red-gold, wipe their frost-bitten eyelids
as if in a fairy tale.
It got cold early.

Winter Village in the High Valley

Eddies on high drift closer,
chase streaks across the window;
a veil flies, whitens the windowpanes;
a curtain falls, the mountain closes
and the land melts away.

Snowflakes interweave, land
on black clods,
rotting leaves;
over the downy blanket a muted whispering;
the dome opens into a swarm
of stars drifting into the cosmos.

The cold creeps in after midnight
with its grinding and crackling.
Splinters of crystal flash
from roofs, between fences—

not a soul anywhere—

moonshadows eavesdrop
on the stillness in graves and yew trees,
lanterns and sunken barns.

APPARENTLY

Where there are two eyes
there is already a face:
in wood, under snow, in stone;
vibrating shadows, whiffs of dust:
We see eyelashes
under the brows of dead leaves.

Obedient matter has fantasy,
eyes that seem alive, frozen or spirited,
observe you,
roll and blink,
squint and wink,
read the hourglass.
What, though, is the other,
second face that someone
allows to ripen
under the mask
of old age?

Snow-Music

Spins, flows, layers itself,
crackles and grows, frozen, crystallized.
Fall as stars to the earth,
interweave, stick, crackle and grind.
The animals sleep,
the people, the soil and grass.
Only the spaces awaken,
listen, learn to hear
the whispering and hush
of the wind's stillness over the snow.

A Music called Snow

Eyes shut, listening in.
You're part of the swell,
hear the whispering of snowflakes.
Flakes are bedding down together
that there may be a new earth—
a swarm settles,
grasped by the wind under its wings.
Breathing-sounds,
whispering and humming.
That old dark music.

Actually, I don't hear a thing.
I feel my pulse in my fingertips,
sense an emptiness in my head, the space
surrounding words whose meanings were lost.

Somehow the fundamental tone remained. Fundamental tones stay.
A wordless snowing—as a couple
who love each other,
move into tomorrow's down.

In the Counter-light

Still empty, but not bare,
the silhouette betrays
the swelling under the bark,
boughs veer off in tiny angles
from the straight line,
branches begin to breathe,
grow towards you in the balmy rain,
germination revealed by pustule and nub.

Step closer, stretch yourself, and bow.
Trees want
to show you their buds.

Waiting-looking contrary to the light, sensing
the wavy line of the awakening wood,
the blood flow of grey-skinned
March! Damp-cool warmth.
It thaws.

THE LAST SPRING

Since my eightieth year
each spring is my last,
sorrow obscures the translucent
blood-young leaves.
Blinded, I turn
from the blooming cherry tree—, return back,
glance upward into a sky of blooms;
a flash of sun, soundless,
soaks in flooding light
a terrain suffocated for weeks;
landscape becomes land,
an instant becomes time,
I am present within,
2 o'clock, early afternoon
at the window over the garden,
its winter bleakness suddenly radiates.

Light warms in the icy air
when memory bursts
in one illuminated moment.

EXISTENCE

Our existence between stars
whose distance feigns beauty
in insurmountable emptiness,
cosmic pseudo-bodies, balls of gas and poison,
stony death-moons
in a veil of reflections,
enchanting illusions
that govern the heartbeat,
women's menstruation,
the tide and ebb of oceans.
We are creatures of a cosmic physicist,
released into fields of gravity,
haunted by the longing
for dark energy,
we subsist at the beck and call
by virtue of the inborn dream
of a light
we don't endure,
that we carry within,
that carries us—
the unendurables.

The Blue Bird

Blue: invented by a god,
casting from afar,
always further,
a bird
out of eternity into time.

Lost Words – Lost World

WORDLESS

I often linger in wordlessness
as if in an empty mussel;
somewhere there is sound,
but I couldn't tell you
from where.

LOST WORDS

If you forget the names
of people and places
from one moment to another,
chaos swallows you.
Who are you? A wisp of straw
still not ready
to slink off out of time,
eaten up by the fire,
swallowed by the pits,
to be pulled apart
by the invisible ghouls
of the earth, your great love
always so alien,
so magnificent and so gruesome.
You, a ghost in a shirt,
devoid of any consolation, threadbare
in the foggy night,
where the moor recognizes you
and calls you by your childhood name,
knows words, lost ones, old ones
such as *Munderloh*, *raw*—the Nobody
in the reeds whispers,
what I no longer comprehend,
that syllable, *glad.*

THE NIGHT

We come from within the night,
try to find a way back into the night,
fall victim to her,
she who sucks us up and spits us out.

Stalk upon stalk burned-out, sound upon sound
mutes the voices of animal and man;
towering higher, the clouds disintegrate,
are the grey alien mountain
behind the mountain, that we know of
since the arms of Mother
lifted us into the starry sky.
How close the stars, how big
the world on the other side of the world.

Blue darkens, dark becomes blue.
That which held in
feelings and visions during daytime,
dissolves; the night is borderless,
the other, the ancient, the secluded dark,
when it snatches us back
to the very point that released us
for a fleeting glimpse, a single breath
in time, in timelessness, truth and deception,—
bleakness and foliage,
hate and life, love and death,
brilliance, reflection, and dust.

THE NIGHT POEM

The written landscape is not
the real landscape: it's more,
sired and born
in a room inside the mind,
and also in sleep, the spirit breath
circulating, an alien light, dream of death.
It's similar to the true memory, reminds of it,
surpasses it, undermines it, lives—
a realm of visions, perception
is a picture, tender and wild,
enigmatic
in its natural state,
quite close and yet far,
is prepared of late
to become a world that remains longer
than a world seen in fate.
That clarity of height and the Earth's fumes.
Over a time, those that read it
call it art; and that, too, dark energy.
It also nourishes he whom it nurses,
when pointing out the resemblance to itself,
fingers our thorns and crowns,
breathes on what we can't comprehend - - -
- - - - - - - - - - - - - - - - - - -
I'm talking about here, where we live,
animal and man, to delight in and to toil,
secretly eloquent
in our oldest, voiceless zones
concealed within their own soil.

[To Georges Wenger]

Can't pray anymore;
in my sleep I stepped on my own grave.

Your paintings accompany me here and there,
help me remain native. They're still a place.

Fought, in pain,
with this poem.
Can't find it anymore,
carry it unremembered in my heart.
Sometimes, as if between flickering shadows,
a word, an image,
your voice. It arrives from afar.
What we once had
hid itself in rhymes.
Once again,
minute and tender,
quite a different way than the world.

The winter woman says:
Those who freeze should love themselves,
count owls and finches as those who still dwell.

In lines and colors:
your paintings too. Labels of the soul,
understand them well; they are you:
skill and knowledge and courage.
I live with them.
Art is mastery and servitude.
I thank you, dear friend,
for your trees, indestructible spaces
in time from which we arise,
into which we fall; the doors locked;
they lead in and out
of your pictures
in the innermost house. What is the soul?
We read and look, understand little
of the work; just the skin and the heart see ...

WRITING

In a forest that has no end,
on a search for myself, poaching,
examining and delineating.
Life—a conversation in pictures.
Where is the word? Where, pencil and paper?
With one who has found himself?
With the other who has lost himself?

Regression

The more I know,
fear to know,
the fainter the desire
to face the unknown,
thirsty for life as before:
as if there were a forest where almost all paths
end in a thicket of thorns
and darkness.

AGE

Dims your eyes, fixed on near and far,
distorts faces, muddles your vocabulary,
clogs your ear, mutes
birdsong, but not the roar of cars.
Ever duller, the house of the finches,
at times a sound from afar,
a direction that can't be pinpointed.
The thunderclap, yes, that still reaches you,
and startles, even when you hear it
as an echo of thunder which once
smashed you down like sledgehammers.
Strange this jerking and flickering
of silent flashes called sheet lightning,
between, then over and behind the clouds—
nothing to do with you—flashes
of another district; on your arthritic
twisted fingers
you count the storm's distance:
300, 600 meters, the discharge is already far off.
But don't deceive yourself
should not a single stalk stir,
not a sound arise from the fields,
and the forest a graveyard,
when the cats sleep and
the birds are silenced, the lightning bolt hits,
and the wavering fire bursts down the deflector,
drives a demon into the earth.

Age—of wisdom? It was prophesied
as solace and consolation, yet not even a hint;
instead of wisdom, you have to learn to endure your
own manner of folly: forget words, sag
into sleep at dinner, while reading, not remembering
names of villages, rivers, old acquaintances, friends,
yesterday's weather—
and what was it called now? that tree
behind the house that you loved.
Books stand all over the place,
the wind carried off the tales they tell,
mixed them beneath the waves in some body of water.
By night it reaches you, pours forth from you,
those forgotten noises from your own Stone Age.

To be old, carrying a crucifix, like poison weeds spurting from the earth
everywhere, on all sides, to confuse you;
still you can swallow, flap, wobble.

An old coin is valuable,
an old chronicle is valuable,
and a crocheted collar is highly valued,
as is the most ancient iron crown
of a ruler from mythical times.

Little valued and decidedly irritating
is the old person,
at least when he's sick
no one wants him.
When he's disposed of,
friends and family
are rid of that smell, the bones and colon,
all discarded,
and that mute discourse with death snuffed out.

THE DEAD HOUR

Between 4 and 5 in the morning.
In an oppressive mood from the day before
because I was quashed
by declarations.
Frozen, the tears
seal the vision tight.

To the pessimist
the evil star appears under
dense cloud.
Fear is chaotic—
not to be of this Earth anymore—
particle within an atom
in a torn-down-to-Nothing-
belonging-to-no-one Everything.

EARTHSTORY

Earth, renewed herself
every hour,
Earth, elfin-young and quagmire-old,
lava-glowing
and tomorrow, dead-cold.

SUCH IS THE DAY

I go, wait, lie down.
Everything once again, once again—
the illness is always right.
Hours pass like this, such is the day
that I will terminate
in foolish hope
that tomorrow it will be better, tomorrow
when the snow melts
and the crows perch
on dripping branches
in front of a heavy sky
who offers no help.
Once I could pray:
Others do it for me today.
Do you think the God of the astronomical universe
has an ear for human stammers?

When suffering, one becomes a child or an animal,
one creeps consoled in a dream
of the hell-meadow, if crow's
head, beak, body,
all point dead ahead into the morning breeze.

The Breath of the *Horae*

That one can hear it only now,
the breath of the *horae*:
Didn't you know
you were born to die!

O yes, I knew, but didn't feel it,
saw what I lived, augmented
by the rays rising and down to the bedrock,
saw what secretly and unfathomably shines,
ridiculed and promised
from mouth to mouth,
the science of coasting over death,
towards a survival outside time.

Everything finished. Wiped.
Like chalk from a chalkboard.
Pale grey slate, a stone in pieces,
but language and writing still not lost;
I still practice my characters and scribbles,
hear the echoes breathing,
want to understand the syllables of birds,
don't want to enter the better world,
beg the pain
to give me the word that hits home.

Nemo

GLASS

There is the glass mountain, the glassy heart,
the little tree that wanted glass leaves.
Simply fairy stories. The one about the love goblet is true,
the one about the death goblet is true. Each of them non-
transparent glass.

OVER THE HILLS AND FAR AWAY

Splinters of lost words
handed through the grille of sickness.
Complete the message with what
you once knew of me.

I'll never become whole again.
Pass me your hand, Mother;
I dreamt *they* were grinning, trying
to catch me. Over the hills and far away ...
someone says: men call it
dance of death.

On the 36th Anniversary of
My Mother's Death, 20th August, 2008

3 a.m. at night, I stand
on the threshold to the room where Mother died.
The white animal under the table
is a blotch of moonlight.
I step closer. The moondeer
doesn't flinch. Nothing moves.
The moon-courtyard is opaque. From the east,
a shoal of fishes
sailing far from the Earth don't recognize me,
know nothing—
nor one from another. Wandering
without return on the moonclear
sky.

From their day corners, their night nests,
the small and smallest creep out,
the winged, the sneaking and swarming
from Oberon's flowing cape,
they gnaw, saw, are among themselves,
destroying and begetting,
making true those sayings
of Die and Become, when the guest listens,
companion to the mooncreature
that appears to stir when he reaches for a breath—
from within: the voice
of the dead mother.

THE DREAM

In a nameless mountain,
a conically narrowing shaft
like a tunnel
in which I look for an eye of light,
a possible exit,
but there's no light,
just a blind pupil, a glass pane in grey night,
always further ahead—
and behind,
nowhere in sight.

IRRITABLE COLON

In the sinister hour, at night
between two and three, alone
in a cell in the old house.
From the corners and hanging in the stuffy air,
the grinning of masks, grimaces
that are and are not, hating me,
taunting me. Deathly still.
At the same time there's a roar within me
as if from a shattering hail. To save myself,
I think of blood, bones, life—
ghouls do their rounds,
I'm incurably sick:
such is the doctor's decree.—
In the transom window morning arrives,
gruesome to me, lurid.
However it may be—life—
life is sad.

DESPERATION

How can I face the morning,
when toward four o'clock,
in debilitating pain
straight out of the world's deathpits,
death ambushes me.

An Early Morning in Daylight-Saving Summer

In a razor-sharp buzzing they come to haul me
from my bat-infested nightmare-time—
of which they, inextricably entwined,
are just as much a part.
The zombies and snouted moths, surveyors of pits,
scuttlers, wriggling animal specters,
lustful sinister scum, the thousand-furred,
tails dragging, hair matted, nameless, working
with forceps and hammer-feet, claws grinding,
scratching, swarming and whirring—
messengers of the twilight find
the nightly bread and, from their sleeping hole,
they drop—Oberon's twilight apparatus—
right into my expiring hand
on the edge of the bed.

I still live. Spread my fingers,
cannot wake up, banished
into the vicious circle of a dream:
And how they come running,
those 13-legged spiders
across their finely spun house of the dead—
and where do the anonymous black tortoise-beetles
on wheels come from? On the curtain three dark tents
are moths, seemingly dead; over the mountain
a strip of yellow: the morning wasteland lies horizontal.
In the twilight the vermin stir.

Some are sucked back into the nightmare;
those that remain dive into cracks—
I jolt awake, remember, wide-eyed, that it was
a summer night's dream. On the window pane
towards daylight,
the day fly, alone, fragile.

The Antagonist

No one knows him by his face.
Like the squirt in the farce,
he sneaks in—
and you fall,
a pain in your leg and blood in your face,
tripped by the lopsided memory stone.

Forfeiting and daring, hush and talk.
No, you didn't know that,
that man shatters just as easily under truth
as under a lie.

Sick in spirit—our friend ensured
he was indeed, feigning it
so he wouldn't have to make himself live it:
"I live the knowledge in seconds;
the antagonist makes his plan,
ambushes me—
his grin face-on,
taps me on the shoulder, a figurine,
he glances at his watch
quite correctly and congenially."

Dark Angel

Everyone knows him,
he with the many faces and voices,
but no one has seen him—
the doctors call him Panic—
when he flaps those raven feathers,
enfolds you from behind
in his steely quills in those dark games.

Which rustling of feathers is that in the starless night?
The deathwind, said the old woman,
latching windows and doors, waking—
it seemed to her, throughout the night, she slept awake,
but in the early gloom
found she was unaware of any dream—
forlorn like a mother-soul and clasping the sentence
she had started out with,
on a forgotten island.

"They snatched my young child
from the cradle."
Eight words; she counted, tried
counting to come back to earth—
until, after unearthly time,
she recognized things within eyeshot, within reach,
that helped her to go on living:
sewing basket, threads and the glass;
and in that glass three weeds
preparing to bloom.

Fear of Death: Rhymes

Those who stand outside
in the frost-pallid night,
peer through dark panes:
Wasn't someone there writing?
Wasn't a light on all night long?

Fool. Trees can't see, can they?
Trees, you believe, see well, gain strength,
donate their limbs
for flowers, leaves and dim shadows.

Flowers illuminate by their own light,
the house's threshold is broken,
rubbed out forever, my face.

Stumbling upon my own borders,
I loose words, an image of myself and courage.
The trees beam, the cloud rests;
hear the soundless scream on the steps,
withered in the rooms
that once saved me
from myself.

FEAR, 21 LINES

Fear we're born with,
because it terrifies us to be pushed out
of the warm
sheltering shadows of the womb,
forbidden to go near the nurturing well,
to be exiled
into the glare, into the cold.

How is fear transformed
into confidence, into trust?
Dependence in devotion?
How, Mother! Child! How
does the eye adjust to the world-
baring light?
And how does that naked sense of being-there
grope for life? How too does life feel love,
and does the soul, when happiness grazes you, yearn,
shudder back into the dark?

How else might we tolerate, uncomprehending—
as blissful as we are anxious—
to be children of death
for a whole lifetime?

The Companion

He waited for me
at the front door,
my school companion.
He whistled as Father whistled
while pulling asparagus
when he wanted a bottle of beer—

All at once he fell upon me, Nemo, the wind,
clutched me under my cloak,
tugged at my scarf,
smacked my cap from my head,
threw himself against breast, forehead, mouth,
breathed in a kiss
that tore into blood and bones,
life and death.

I got old, you stayed young;
flew by the latched window,
when I hear you whispering, you wave with branches,
when you're invisible, you teach
eavesdropping and silence.

Soon I'll sleep
lullaby wind, soon you'll be a draft in a locker
when the woman I was
mulls over letters
and crumbling papers
she thought lost.

THE EXTINGUISHING

That red-golden flame
withering to blue flickers.
The flickers waver,
grieve in the still wind,
a trembling dot
in the suffocated dark,
colorless terminal point, roaring stillness.
Who on earth hears a heart that screams.
Those whom it reaches, harken to their own
as if it were alien.
God is present in loyal absence.

Dark energy,
black-heart life.
White flames fly towards me.

Last Hour

Perhaps you lie there alone
in a cell
for the moribund,
in a deathly sweat but ice cold,
perhaps one of the women
who one once could call
sister, accompanies you
into the labyrinth of tunnels
to that giant night;
once, when—shimmering gold, ore in angel form—
the gate gleamed,
and you lie parched, speechless,
powerless to raise a syllable,
an in-between thing of sheer horror,
dust to dust,
gasping, expiring spark upon spark
like a fire in a dying oven;
at night between two-thirty and three
when the sky
in the icy night
is burning with stars
and no cloud cover
protects you from the blinding,
they say, eternal, light.

Autumn Guest

So silent so silent the November night
that I hear the dreary wind
fumbling
around my bed.
He breathes on my clothes,
grazes shoes and caps—
all of it, he says,
you don't need it anymore,
then packs the stuff in a sack.
Shouldering the sack,
he exits through the wall—
I still manage to clutch on
to my handkerchief
(tears run inside of me),
recognize, with dry eyes,
my room on this side
of the sad dream—
I remind myself
to forget it
in writing.

An Area
of Shadows
Ernst Halter

After the tempest, death star Sun
breaks through the clouds,
blazes, hovers,
touches Earth, disintegrates
to embers, extinguishes until night
settles on the face of day.

Rearguard action of lightning
over breathing trees,
the mortal, most powerful dreams on earth—
the heat is quenched
and stillness floods back—

Eyes emptied, burnt out
to the gloom in your absence.
Day won't ever come back to you.
Not a word remains with you, no flower,
not even your face, as a reminder
of this great attempt to live.

7.10.2010

Tempest and host of winds,
the days blur into a bloom.
Prodding step by step with the umbrella,
you feel your way down into the garden
clenching the last tulips shut,
your glance through shoes to child and grave,
sparse phrases, "look"—"ah, leave it",
language is lost to us,
as the unsaid grows over our voices.

5.10.2008

Let no one see them
at the kitchen sink, at the cat bowl—
an assault, pain, happiness,
they dribble for you and for me
and don't delude themselves.
How salty we are—
we carry the sea with us.
Let them pour, until the eyes
are emptied for a glimpse into the void.

5.10.2008

HOUR OF TRUTH

What is the hour?
The gloaming.
He shakes ashes through the fire grill
with clammy hands.
There's the mug
she drank from as a child,
and over there a pair of worn-out shoes
she wore all summer.
That was it. Was that all?
Time plucks sand.

How small and pale she slept,
hunched over her lump of pain,
in that mountain of pillows under oxygen
with her morphine.
For always? No one knows. Ah, leave it.
He doesn't believe a word,
everyone speaks
as soon as her mouth shatters in the scream
with its hollow echo.

From the winter window through the black
linden tree he sees the fog coursing
in the valley, the lake on the moor,
mountains of glass and shards:
mother-island, father-continent.
Just give her a single day in the ancestral home
with a clear view of the wide horizon and the land!
Who gives? Who takes?
"Never" must be forbidden!

He clears away the plates, the cups, the cutlery,
as if she had died yesterday.
How she loved to live
as light ray and mirror, selfish yet approachable,
and clothes in seven closets.
Only that last item missing.
Now she's often going astray and complains,
she who awakened a voice in the youngsters
and offered her hands freely—
now, no one takes her by the hand.

A burst of morning breaks through the clouds.
He shudders: ice and light—
and turns away to his task.
Time grinds sand.

12.9.2009

The objects are quite still,
the air is motionless.
They were always still,
I hear them only since you've gone away.
The day blurs, the outlines waver,
I have cataracts,
the windows are bars.

I walk upstairs into your room
and listen for the childbreath of your sleep,
but the stillness yawns in every step,
closes at the back against the wall.
No echo remembers.
These objects deny me their glances.
I can't find sleep.
Hermetic mourning.

11.15.2009

Dawning, Darkening

Caught in a web of spring fog,
I stoke the glowing coals.
You wouldn't freeze
if you were to return home today.
You wait, I wait.
The black kite whistles
through the clawing white cold: *Never! Never!*
The fox winds through the thicket,
the larch crowns are in their winter skins—
yet in the branches, a coin is turning blue.

Sun's fires ice over
during my introspective teatime:
your animals in the cloud book,
fishes, sheep, chimeras,
my clowns in the fir trees.
Fog floods the moor,
creeps up the hill.
Are you awake? Asleep?
I turn on the light.
The night is a tunnel.

1.19.2010

The bells in the tower strike eight
all through the vibrating night,
I lie here and wait.
The living have to adapt
to their pressing tasks,
and I learn patience.

If only I could write you
just seven words of love,
yet the type stumbles over its own limbs,
meaning loses itself in the dimmed tracks.

The rhymes tease and fool me,
ring out from God knows where,
are drowned trees
in a rising sea.

Exiled, extinguished, forgotten,
I have to drink and eat
and pile it on, year after year.
They cleanse me, wash me, bed me,
I am my own child;
if only someone knew what kind.

12.25.2009

You wait three thousand hours
from dusk until the dawn
alone with yourself in the house of death,
you rein in fears
until a nurse arrives
to unwind you from the pain.
You sketch the gruff orderly,
search for paper, pencil, tablets
and wander along the traces,
the distant suns of your childhood,
back all those years.
Our mothers sitting
at ease under the apple trees.
Without hope you scare yourself awake,
and you feel old and cold.
The dark fiddler at the end of the bed
sits up with you, and you grant him
one last game with words and rhymes.
When night falls, he falters, and I
hesitantly enter your exile.

5.10.2010

God is a dark spot.
If only he were a star,
I don't see him.
What can I mean to him?
Don't leave me, my love, all alone.
Is there such a thing as nothingness?
I must know,
the heaviest hour approaches.
Are we the crash of a wave,
a spark tossed through dark space
from here to the Pleiades?

I would like snow,
a last white sea,
and far on the horizon
the burning of the shores where I once lived.
Then, you can let me sleep.

2.17.2010

Come Bird-Sleep!
Bundle her in your wings,
carry her away from medicines and mattresses,
unravel her bonds,
open your dark gate for her,
take her by the hand.
Lead her a last winter's lap,
snow and night in her hair,
through your borderless land.

12.31.2009

My knees buckle,
I pull myself together,
clammy fingers and stiff hands.
You, my beloved, my longing,
I torture myself through objects—
and they ask me
to be brave.

12.25.2009

MARIE GRUBBE

Your horizons:
apple trees, coolly
lighting up the rising night.
The sun's northwest country,
the quarters of the dead.
One was consumed by illness;
the other threw himself into darkness.
Voices stalk you
and the lonelier you become,
shadows close in on you like people.
See this last meadow of blooming poppies
leaning towards blue,
stroked one last time
by the red wind
blowing through your straw hat and lace.

Now against your will, in your old person's shack,
against the scrubbed wall,
you in your wheelchair
spooning shame and indignity,
Marie Grubbe.

8.22.2010

Hunched in your bed of exile,
coughing words—
in glass and bowl,
virtually blind hands
wipe slime from the mouth.
The eyes wander astray.
Who's waiting for you
in the twilight between flowers and wall?
Embrace you—I don't dare.
Your bones burn under your skin.

How did he move towards you?
With the mask and majesty
of your face from over there?

4.22.2010

I guard your breathing,
I call the name.
Do you still hear me?
I sit up with you, nod off, startle awake,
count the heartbeats.
I see you on the first day
in the radiation of the longest evening.
Now you lie contorted
in the last night.
Our frailty—you,
our love—you,
our beauty and sadness—you.
I am advised, what it means
to be human:
a borderless point
when we step through.

4.12.2010

Not the arm around you,
not your hand in mine,
cheek against cheek—
you wander,
seek your way
out of fear and morphine
over ground and chasm.
If I could be your handkerchief
or that blue stone you clasp—
still the earth holds you fast.

4.12.2010

Hiatus

Coughing, heckling,
damp bony hands;
the eyes, blind slits,
yet the heart still thumps on
in the monitor, time.
Midday light from the window, bells ringing,
a pair of birds in the tree.
What was in the room? What is it?
You, head downcast, you are
done,
and not a dying word,
how everything ends
and where.

Your body a relic
before me, before the blank wall
of silence where the tears run down.
Now you are
what never completes a thought:
whether duration,
whether destination.
Grief attaches itself to a corpse.

5.24.2010

With their angelic patience for the handicapped,
they are happy to explain how one dies.
They recite, in their wisdom,
that everything was and is and will be as predicted:
the faltering breathing,
the stopping of the heart
when the liver and the brain give up
and the eyes glaze over.
Without exception, nature's laws in motion:
Now the body temperature sinks to room temperature;
a last surge of fever: the putrefaction,
new beginnings for bacterial blooms.
Her solace is without doubt.
And when a quake engulfs a city,
it makes itself known on the fingers of the left hand.

Someone throws himself over the body
that once was life and now is death.

5.3.2010

You with me at the table for this hour—
your local eternity.
I eat and drink to the night.
Does your absence torment you?
Does my voice cause you pain?
How you went missing!
And I have to wait, where we touched.
At the coffin, on your cold lips,
I did believe once, twice,
in eternal life.

2.24.2010

Your legacy—
clothes boots caps pencil books.
Where to put them?
You jam the stairway and block
the doors with your absence.
And with every place and hour
feeling their tenderness,
when it was part of you:
That black-and-white coat
in the winter of my new ice skates.
You calling from the shore: Come!
Frosted fur and blond hair,
black wings spread wide.
Two children laughing mouth on mouth.

The fog's stillness—
smoke—
a hair.
The death.

4.26.2010

What we survive—
what survives you:
The things that once lay in your hands
sleep on
and serve to change sleep;
the lover wears your most beautiful dress.
On her body, it follows
the breath and the voice
as long as the years draw on.

What remains yours is the handwriting,
the books, every letter,
pages scribbled full
with the death-child's
broken words
from the pit of exile.
And wandering tracks
through my foggy chamber
remind me
of your burnt-out radiance.

2.4.2010

In the last year, the little wishes:
After our tea, around six,
slowly, arm in arm, a walk in the garden,
bell sky, fragrance of elderberry trees,
an eternity of sparkling butterflies,
picking a bunch of tulips,
stem by stem, plucked with force,
and *lilies without, roses within,*
like Marvell's complaint.
Fashion catalogues, and in the evening, *Foehn* wildlife,
in the day's awakening, the outline and call
of the messenger bird.
Pencil and notepad,
the word through walls,
reports from the still bedrock.
A cashmere jacket,
your golden opera shawl
and, at night, the slippers
that were incinerated with you.

4.24.2010

"It's insufficient—"
the law for those that remain.
The dead are ahead of us,
we have that gazing
into the skies, sleep or nothingness.
Death has made these noble.
Her peaceful rest out of time.
They don't have to do anything;
we, everything.
With wide eyes they see
unknown rays from the skies.
And we hammer our hands
blind and bloody
on clear crystal.

4.30.2010

Made your bed under a vacant moon,
pillow under pillow,
steadied the sagging head,
kissed you warm,
kissed you cooled,
the difference, 30 degrees—
life.
Everyone—no one knows.
God without man—dead word,
a mistake of his creation.—
Has snow fallen tonight? No snow:
The moon is full.

4.25.2010

After you, **I am**
the same and another.
I feel as if I walked with you
through the fire.
Me?
You—ashes without resurrection
and I am still whole,
the grain-child, all the recklessness
burned up.

In your backcountry
I was only a blind guest.
Surely you saw me,
I didn't see you,
there was nothing to touch,
I heard no footsteps,
found no tracks in the sand,
and climbed back into the light.
I live.

5.3.2010

I touch the sleeve of your death dress;
one gives the dying back what's theirs.
The floral lace gripped your wrist
where the pulse was buried,
the drumbeat on the horizon
withdrawing every hour.

Cloth in hand, no resistance,
one heartbeat only.
Give me sleep, I beg of you.

5.7.2010

"My love, don't leave, I beg of you.
Don't leave!" for the second, third time.
I slammed the door and fled,
out of reproach, anguish and lament,
my bewildered tears.
The streets were ice and murk,
shadows of decades;
at home, the bread and wine were frozen.

The rapeseed, signal-yellow in a cold bloom;
the sun bakes in the images.
Your infant hands twitch in mine:
"Don't leave. I beg of you."
I fled,
the walls speechless,
hour upon hour I catch up
with myself, alone.

5.8.2010

Deathzone

You were immodest, wanted
a loving heart for you alone—
they divided their hearts
among seventy nicely modest inmates—
you gave gifts,
they felt it was a bribe—
they nudged the full plate towards you
and wished you bon appétit,
you had none, searched
for eyes that looked at you—
from the kitchen, from the street
their voices broke in on you,
you stammered—
their duties led them day and night,
you had one only—and its deadline unknown.
For them death was an average value
like the flu;
you hoped for the last trace of light.
I came and went and wrote away the tears.
I said nothing.

6.4.2010

Your final, thousand-and-first photo,
on a blister pack
with the tablets rustling inside
for the last of your nineteen weeks
in this hospice of the dying.
Two to be taken in the morning, one in the evening,
the window, *Monday 7-9*,
has broken through.
The telephone call when they asked where to let you die
came at three-thirty in the afternoon.

Terror and laughter contort your face,
imprecise, zero contrast, the eyes buttons,
even the red shawl,
your guardian and comfort: blur.
Pillows prop you,
in the right hand, a pencil twitches,
last weapon
for defense against such imposition.

A mug shot on room twozerofour,
so you wouldn't be confused
with an insane person.

5.9.2010

Your future is exhausted,
mine is deferred,
and day after day I have to take
the night path with you.
I'm too fleeting—
gravity knows no light.
I serve myself those last pictures,
you were never as much yourself,
as you were in the house of torment.
I didn't follow you
into the land of For-Always-Or-Never.
Today the first poppies bloom.

5.16.2010

Bell flowers,
slender blue towers
on the edge of the forest,
leaning into the sun—
I turned back.
I broke them off for you,
brought them to the sleeping one at her bed.
You opened your eyes.
Even now I hear your joy.
You're like day, like night around me—
they are not meant for hands,
but deep within me.

6.19.2010

On the first new moon after your death-moon
the land slips—as we move through her—
with time and suffering through days and nights,
under the older light.
You brought me four fates—
and I was still a child yesterday.
How light you weigh in my hand.
Starlings occupy the trees,
the hawthorn blooms over you,
the house divides the clouds.
You sleep within me.

5.14.2010

You, consumed by the fire,
my hunger has remained true.
Your smile drowned in the Ganges
a shimmer, a shadow, a nothing.
And life carries me on.
Our time returns to me,
the inexplicable light
when in the night we invented
the childhood we wished for one another,
invented flowers and castles.
Flocks of swallows fish the sky empty.
Do you know more?—
"We're walled in,
chirping and whirring,
birds without flight."
Tears—
and I understand nothing.

8.1.2010

Your pullover in the north wind
flaps his sleeves,
swings his waist,
shakes his collar.
You're coming. You're returning!
I jolt out of the waking,
a step to the side and the vision
sweeps through the dead forests,
trunk by trunk, grown
out of our expired days.

9.6.2010

Now an invisible stranger
rises into his steps
echoing down the empty stairs.
Now the sentences in his head ask of
the silence toward love and guilt.
He hears his own voice
speaking on the tape:
Will return soon from the trip.
Please have patience.

Now, for the first time, he investigates closets and rooms,
observes his fingers in amazement.
Now his suffering radiates life and courage,
and he mourns mourning.
And thus he writes himself ahead and further on,
travels through the night to the one,
embraces her white gift,
dives and swims on into the rest of time.
No place anchors him in the flood, not yet.

14.6.2010

Still snow and sun,
storm and rain house,
but the horizon is empty
where you turned around and severed
the todays from the tomorrows.
All around, the landscape stretches
into the mourning
of a dream from some-no-where,
no dawn, no dusk,
drifting, unhinged shadows.
In the window of your early years
clouds pile up red, like childhood.
The evening hills are grown over,
I walk them darkly and alone,
I learn the tenderness of everyday words
like room, lamp, wine,
and practice a woman's touch
as if arms were wings.
Let it be attempted.

5.3.2010

THE OUTSIDER

Hourly clang of a clocktower,
stairs, gate, a light,
in the light, a white sprig of blooms,
a house, a block in brown city smog,
the gable hunts clouds,
the windows, eyes of the blind
who were once seeing:
blank and night.
What is this place called?
He leans on the railing.
Where did the street branch off
after this loneliness?

Was it not *she* who lived here long ago?
Did he not climb up the stone ledges
like a child and gaze at her?
Doesn't a shy shadow flow high
up the hill's slope and bring him
what he wasn't searching for?
That he must wait here in the darkness
in front of Father shaft and Mother grotto,
her red chamber of love:
the last of this house,
outsider once again.
Came from afar—and everything comes down to him.

5.20.2010

You mutate to an icon
contrary to knowledge and facts.
Your accouterment of
a miracle-working Madonna,
the thousand furs for Nobile and Nansen ,
Emma Bovary's shawls,
the photo albums of one Grace and one Liz—
your gifts for the needy.

You don't need all of that anymore.
You princess on the pea,
wafted here by the black wind of the sun,
descended into the ash urn.
Your apparition makes dreams bleed red.
I look back at you through time
and show you to no one.

8.29.2010

Insubstantial light.
I'm hoping for the evening,
waiting for the hour
when you walk within me
through the stillness of thoughts,
as my voice,
and speak out of the ashes:
"Remember the lament.
It oozes from every living thing
in all the future and
since the beginning of days."

8.15.2010

THE RETURN

Nothing more than an escape
from your white shadow in the night
lies behind me.
Now I stand again where I went,
surprised in autumn.
Chestnuts and corn became blond,
the cherry trees bare,
in every spider web, tattered
silvery coins of *Robinia.*
From the herder's fire, where we sat
high on the mountain, smoke rises.
You glimpse
for the first time since your death
through my eyes into gray November:
How short the day.
How long he seemed to us in that distant
April and May and Julius.
The house remains silent,
on the ground floor a door slams.
Who's there? The wind? An animal?
The nameless.
And right across our waiting,
over there and here,
the blank time cuts coldly
and burns like nothing.

10.17.2010

A pencil under the table
dulled by word-work,
an old breakdown in machine writing,
your red comb,
the pillows of deathly fear.
The sun before its decay,
the outline of your shadow in black leaves.
I watch the flapping of the crows,
from the tired fields to the river.
The water draws and flees
through its mirrors.
The day becomes vague,
the wind yields to the dusk,
light spreads, ash drifts.

10.28.2010

ZERO

The day is the day
unlived
and the night, sleepless.
A word is a word
unsaid,
and speechless the stillness.
Carrots are potatoes are veal
uncooked,
fasting makes no sense.
The death is the death
is the death
untrained,
like the birth.
A red dot
between rib five and six,
left, where the heart
beats against fingers.
Un-atoned is entrance and exit.

12.29.2007

It's said,
and nothing said.
Words remain words.
What gets me is the voice remembered,
not from here,
but the after-echo and obituary
deep out of the last century,
as you, radiating darkly,
stepped in front of my world:
"My love, yours is the way.
Mine is time."

6.24.2010

ERIKA BURKART was born in Aarau, Switzerland in 1922. Throughout her career she published over 24 collections of poetry, 8 prose works, and was awarded numerous literary prizes, including the Conrad-Ferdinand-Meyer-Preis (1961) and the Gottfried-Keller-Preis (1992). She was the only woman ever to have been awarded Switzerland's highest literary prize, der Grosser Schillerpreis (2005). She passed away on April 14, 2010.

ERNST HALTER is a Swiss author and poet who lives in Althäusern, Switzerland. He has been publishing poetry, short stories and novels for over 40 years. Among his most important works are: *Die Stimme des Atems* (*The Breath's Voice*) (2003); *Über Land* (*Overland*), (2007); and the novels, *Das Buch Mara* (*The Book of Mara*), (1988) and *Jahrhundertschnee* (*Snow Century*), (2009).

MARC VINCENZ is Swiss-British, was born in Hong Kong, and currently divides his time between Reykjavik, Zurich and New York City. His work has appeared in many journals, including *Washington Square Review, Canary, The Bitter Oleander*, and *Guernica*. His recent books include *The Propaganda Factory, or Speaking of Trees*; *Pull of the Gravitons*; *Gods of a Ransacked Century*; and forthcoming from NeoPoiesis Press, *Mao's Moles*. A new English-German bi-lingual collection, *Additional Breathing Exercises*, is forthcoming from Wolfbach Verlag, Zurich, Switzerland (2013). His recent translations include *Kissing Nests* by Werner Lutz (Spuyten Duyvil, 2013) and *Secret Letter* by Erika Burkart from Cervena Barva Press.

SPUYTEN DUYVIL
Meeting Eyes Bindery
Triton
Lithic Scatter

www.ingramcontent.com/pod-product-compliance
Lightning Source LLC
Chambersburg PA
CBHW020937090426
42736CB00010B/1168